Steve Parish KIDS

Nature watch
Birds

CONTENTS

Feathered Fliers

Corellas

Birds are special animals that were among the first creatures to be able to fly. Some ancient types of birds even lived when dinosaurs walked the Earth! But although all birds have wings, not all of them can fly. So what other things make birds birds?

Tawny frogmouth

The main things that make birds unlike all other animals are feathers. Birds also have a combined nose and mouth, known as beaks or bills, instead of mouths.

All birds lay eggs. Most baby birds have only a small amount of fluffy feathers when they hatch.

Ibis chick & egg

Imagine that!

Although it may not look like it, a bird's feathers are made of the same type of stuff as your fingernails and hair! Your hair also falls out and regrows, just like a bird moults its feathers.

Swans, like Australia's black swans, have the most feathers of all birds. Adult swans have many thousands of feathers. The shape and size of feathers affects how a bird takes off and how it flies.

Archaeopteryx

The true "early bird"

The first bird, Archaeopteryx, lived hundreds of millions of years ago. Although it had feathers and a wishbone like today's birds, some other parts of its body were more reptile-like.

Black swan

3

Superb fairy-wren

From tiny to towering

Little corellas

Many types of birds live in Australia and some from other countries also visit during the year.

Birds come in all shapes and sizes, from the largest Australian bird, the emu, to the tiny Mallee emu-wren.

Some birds live in large groups called flocks, which can have many thousands of birds. Often an entire flock will sleep, or roost, together in the same place.

Mallee emu-wren

Weebill

The smallest bird

Australia's smallest bird from head to tail is the weebill, which is just 9 centimetres long. Many people think the Mallee emu-wren should be called the smallest. Its body is just 6 centimetres long, but its tail is longer.

Wherever you go, you are likely to see or hear birds, whether they are big or small. Birds live all around Australia.

Australasian gannets

Emus

The tallest bird

The emu is the second-largest bird in the world. Only the ostrich is bigger. Like most very large birds, it is too big to fly. Instead, it walks along pecking up seeds, insects and grass from the ground.

5

Fluffy & warm

Most birds are almost totally covered in feathers. Feathers can have many shapes and colours — some can even glow in the dark!
A bird's feathers may change colour during breeding season or when the bird grows from a chick to an adult.

Contour feather

Baby barn owls

Little penguin

Feathers help keep birds warm and dry. Down feathers are the soft, fluffy feathers often seen on a bird's belly or chest. The long flight feathers are known as "contour feathers". Other feathers, called semiplumes, are part fluffy and part long.

Falling out feathers

As a bird grows, its feathers fall out. This is called moulting. The feathers then grow all over again. For this reason, most baby birds do not look like their parents and have fluffier feathers in a different colour, like the baby booby in this picture. Some even hatch with hardly any feathers at all.

Brown booby & chick

I preen to stay clean.

Birds ruffle up their feathers and use their beaks to peck their feathers clean of lice, dust or dirt. This is known as preening and most birds do it every day.

Plumed whistling-duck

Zebra finch

Preening prettily

Birds keep their feathers clean and stop them from getting tatty by bathing and preening. Some birds, such as ducks and swans, have a type of oil called preen oil, which seeps out of their skin and helps keep their feathers smooth, glossy and water-resistant.

7

What's inside a bird?

Like you, a bird has a backbone, a heart and lungs. But birds have special features that help them to fly and to live. To fly, birds must be very light, so they have hollow spaces in their bones. They also have air sacs that trap air in the body.

Black-naped tern

Bird skeleton

Flying uses up a lot of oxygen and energy (try flapping your arms for a few minutes to see how tiring it is). For this reason, birds have different lungs to mammals. A bird's lungs have more veins connecting them to the heart, and they work much better than yours do.

Bombs away!

Birds' bottoms are a little different to yours too, because birds mate, poo and lay eggs all out of just one hole. They don't need to wee, but they do poo a lot — so look out below!

Spinifex pigeon

8

Straw-necked ibis

Wedge-tailed eagle

Australian pelican

Hot blooded

A bird's body has to stay much warmer than a human's body. It can get very cold high in the air. The bird's fluffy feathers help keep the heat in so it stays nice and warm while flying.

Eastern curlew

Bills & beaks

Different birds have different beaks suited to the type of food they eat. Meat and insect eaters, like magpies and butcherbirds, have pointed beaks for poking about in the ground to find worms or tearing into insect shells.

Parrots and cockatoos use their powerful beaks to crack into nuts and pine cones.

Swans, ducks and other waterfowl have flat, wide bills that act like sieves for searching through the water and snapping up small fish.

Honeyeaters sip sweet nectar from flowers, so they need long, curved beaks that can reach deep into blooms.

Magpie

Eclectus parrot

Black swan

Red-necked avocet

Eastern spinebill

Going Fishing!

The red-necked avocet has a very long beak that is tilted upwards. It uses its beak to poke about for fish in the water just above the bottom of a shallow pond. The beak's tilted shape may help the bird avoid the mud it stirs up as it fishes.

Whistling kites swoop down on small mammals and birds but they are also scavengers that see carrion (dead animals) on the roadside as an easy meal.

Whistling kites

Wedge-tailed eagle

Meat eaters

Eagles, hawks, falcons and ospreys eat meat or fish. They have sharp beaks and claws called talons for tearing into flesh.

Walk on the wild side

A bird's feet also suit its lifestyle. Some birds have webbed feet to help them swim. Others have razor-sharp claws for clutching prey or strong toes suited to scratching up dirt to find food.

The largest group of birds is known as the "perching birds" because they have feet that can grip on to branches to "perch". This group includes finches and some of Australia's most famous songbirds.

Ducks and other waterbirds have webbed feet that act like oars or paddles to push them through the water as they swim.

Plumed whistling-duck

Star finch

Eclectus parrot

Claw-like feet

Cockatoos and parrots have claw-like feet with two toes pointing forwards and two pointing backwards. This helps them grasp on to branches and hold nuts and seeds firmly while they crack them open. They also use their claws for scratching.

Comb-crested jacana

Jacanas and other small waterbirds have long, thin toes that help them "walk on water" so they don't sink on lily pads.

I can walk on water!

Reptile relatives

Cockatoo foot

Birds are distantly related to reptiles. This is the reason birds have scaly feet — just like their ancestors, the dinosaurs, probably had.

Bird brains

For many years, scientists thought birds were not the brainiest of animals, which led to the term "birdbrained". In fact, birds are much smarter than people once thought.

Sulphur-crested cockatoos

The great frigatebird has learnt that it is a lot easier to steal a meal from another bird than it is to catch fish for itself. It attacks other birds in the air and takes their dinner.

Torresian crow

Great frigatebirds

Crows and ravens are known to be very clever. They have been seen using tools, such as sharp rocks or twigs, to help them get into food.

Black-breasted buzzard

Smart egg-smashers

The black-breasted buzzard picks up rocks with its beak and tosses them at other birds' eggs to smash and eat them.

Many birds fly long distances from country to country each year. Once they are able to fly, even the chicks seem to know the way without having ever travelled before. Scientists are puzzled by how these birds find their way.

Splendid fairy-wren

Bar-tailed godwits

Bird musicians

Some songbirds have excellent memories and can remember hundreds of tunes. Songbirds make many sounds, ranging from tweets and twitters to complex melodies that may even include parts of other birds' tunes.

Bird senses

Bush stone-curlew

Have you ever heard the saying "a bird's eye view"? It means to see the big picture or to look down on something the way birds do when they fly. For birds to see while flying high in the sky, they must have very good eyesight. Birds can see many more colours than you can and are able to focus very well.

Letter-winged kite

The letter-winged kite is the only kite in Australia that hunts at night. However, its eyes are more like those of a day-hunting bird so it has to look for prey by moonlight.

Birds such as swiftlets, which live in dark caves, have a special way of hearing that is also used by bats. Swiftlets make clicking noises and then listen for the echoes. This way of hearing and moving around following echoes is called echolocation.

Swiftlet

Barking owl

"Eye" spy

An owl can't move its eyeballs around, **so** it has to move its whole head. Many birds also have a third see-through eyelid that protects their eyes while they fly or dive.

Owls have excellent night vision and can also hear very well. They know exactly where a sound is coming from because one of their earholes is higher on the head than the other. This means they don't have to turn their heads to know where a sound comes from.

What are you staring at?

Barking owl

Silent listeners

An owl can hear noises that are ten times fainter than the noises you can hear. But when an owl moves it can be so quiet that, unless one hooted, you may not even notice it!

Southern boobook

Willie wagtail

Singing sensations

Wherever you are, in the city, bush or beach, you have no doubt heard birds singing. Every species has its own call, which is used to communicate with others and, sometimes, to find a mate. Some birds even know many songs and sing in choirs.

Rufous scrub-bird

Australia's two lyrebird species are both wonderful mimics and great dancers. They can copy all sorts of sounds, including chainsaws, dogs barking and other birds' tunes.

Zz...zz...zzzzzzz...

Woof! Woof!

Superb lyrebird

Songs for all the family

Magpies are among the best singers. They can trill at a number of pitches and know hundreds of tunes. Each magpie creates its own unique song that includes parts of its mum and dad's songs and parts it has invented itself.

Magpie

Golden-headed cisticola

Some famous bird carollers are warblers, larks and cisticolas. Although they look plain, they sing lovely melodies.

Purple-crowned fairy-wrens

Scratch cocky!

Black-cockatoo

Parrots and lorikeets tweet, screech or squawk, but some that live with humans can learn to "talk". Scientists are unsure exactly how they do this because they do not have voice boxes like we do.

Strutting their stuff

Cockatoo

Just like you, birds use body language to "talk" to others of their kind. They may flap their wings, bob their wings or even dance and "strut their stuff".

Brolgas and black-necked storks are graceful birds known for their dancing. When they greet each other, they leap up and down with their large wings outstretched.

Great crested grebes are waterbirds that perform a strange dance at mating time. The male and female shake their heads, give each other a gift of water weeds, then rise up until their chests touch while paddling the water quickly with their feet.

Black-necked storks

Great crested grebes

Crested terns

When crested terns are trying to find a partner, they bring a fish back to the colony and then flap their wings, bob their heads and fly, twirling and soaring together in a spectacular "flight display".

We go on **joy flights** together.

Bowers in blue

Satin bowerbirds even build lovely bowers to dance in to attract females. The bower is not a nest — it is more like a pretty stage for the bird to show off his moves. The male decorates it with blue objects, which match his beautiful blue eyes.

Bowerbird

Eastern rosellas

Dressed to impress

Rather than dancing or singing, some birds use their looks to attract a mate. But what a bird thinks looks nice may seem very odd to you and me!

To attract a mate, the male great frigatebird blows up, or inflates, a large red pouch on his throat, which looks a bit like a big red balloon.

Frigatebird

Australian king-parrots

Female

Male

For most birds, like this male and female Australian king-parrot, the male is more colourful than the female. Sometimes, when birds are ready to make babies, their feathers get even brighter than usual.

Flirting with feathers

Some male birds grow extra long feathers, known as breeding plumes, on the head or chest when it is time to mate and raise a family.

Spoonbill

Who's a pretty boy, then?

Western corellas

When corellas are ready to mate, the feathers on their faces go a pretty pink colour. The baggy skin around their eyes also changes colour to a bright purple-blue.

A feathery headdress

The male great bowerbird grows a bright pink and purple feathery headdress and makes a bower lined with white stones when he is ready to find a female friend.

Great bowerbird

23

Male eclectus parrot

Spotted pardalotes

Building a nest

Once a male and a female bird pair up, it is time to build a nest. Nests can be made out of many things, including twigs, feathers, mud, droppings or even spit!

Female eclectus parrot

Pardalotes tunnel into a creek bed to make a long burrow. So the parents can see the chicks when they fly back to the dark nest, the insides of the chicks' mouths glow in the dark.

Most pigeons and doves build nests from twigs, leaves and soft feathers called down.

Bronzewing pigeons

Apostlebirds build their nests out of caked mud mixed with bird spit.

Apostlebird chicks

One big happy family

Metallic starlings

A whole colony (or group) of metallic starlings all use the same nest. The nest is a huge bunch-like collection of vines, palm leaves and grasses high in the tree tops.

Fairy martin

Mum and dad fairy martins work together to build a bottle-shaped nest out of clumps of mud, lined with grass and feathers. Sometimes hundreds of these nests are clustered together under bridges, eaves of roofs, or overhangs.

Fairy martin nests

Australasian gannet

Black noddy

The best nest?

Fantail

Birds will nest just about anywhere, including on bare ground or in and around human houses and sheds.

Hatching out

Pelican chick

Albatross & chick

Emu chick & eggs

One thing that sets birds apart from most mammals is that birds lay eggs. A baby bird, or embryo, grows bigger inside a hard shell until the egg cracks. The chick then uses a special hard part, or "egg tooth", on its beak to peck its way out.

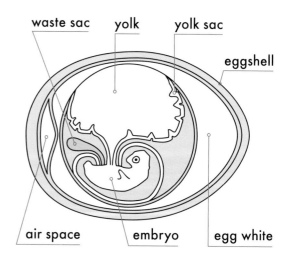

waste sac   yolk   yolk sac   eggshell

air space   embryo   egg white

Until the chick hatches, the egg acts as a small, protective cradle for the baby bird. The yolk, like the one you eat in a hen's egg, is not the baby — it is the chick's food.

A very big omelette!

The emu egg is the largest bird egg found in Australia. It is the size of a large mango and can weigh more than 700 grams — that's more than a whole carton of hen's eggs.

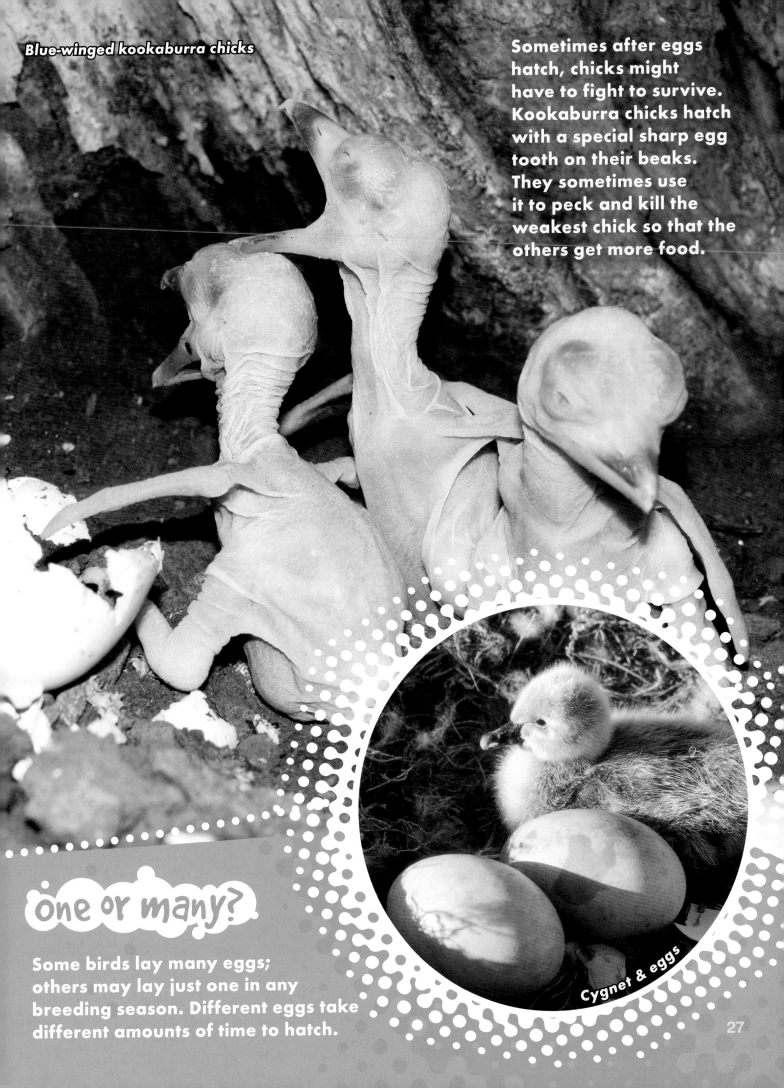

Blue-winged kookaburra chicks

Sometimes after eggs hatch, chicks might have to fight to survive. Kookaburra chicks hatch with a special sharp egg tooth on their beaks. They sometimes use it to peck and kill the weakest chick so that the others get more food.

Cygnet & eggs

one or many?

Some birds lay many eggs; others may lay just one in any breeding season. Different eggs take different amounts of time to hatch.

Eurasian coots

An egg hatching

Chew & spew

Apart from a chick's egg tooth, which falls off shortly after a baby bird hatches, birds don't have any teeth. Most baby birds can't fend for themselves, so bird parents may have to find a way to make their babies' food easy to swallow.

White-eared honeyeater

Many baby birds cannot fly for weeks or even months after they hatch. Most also cannot eat the same food the adults eat. Often, the parents go and find food, eat it, and then spew it up into their chicks' mouths later.

Barn owl chicks

Nice mice for tea

When the chicks get a little bigger and start to grow feathers, their parents might bring them prey and start to teach them how to hunt for themselves.

I eat chewed up fish right out of Mum's beak!

Masked booby & chick

Red-tailed tropicbird & chick

Under the Wing

Either the mother or father bird, or in some cases both, may care for the eggs and chicks until they are old enough to look after themselves. They keep the babies warm under the wing, feed them and teach them how to fly and hunt for food themselves.

Staying safe

Tropicbirds

Baby birds are very helpless until they can fly. For this reason, they are often preyed upon by meat-eating animals, including other birds. Bird parents have many tricks and tactics to protect their chicks from their enemies.

Brown goshawks

Birds of prey build their nests, which are called eyries, high in the tree tops where they will be safe from snakes.

Bush stone-curlews

Bush stone-curlews put on a display of flapping, squawking and dive-bombing if anything tries to eat their chicks. The parents also pretend to be injured to lure predators away.

Tern rookery

Safety in numbers

Living in groups helps birds protect their babies. Breeding colonies, or rookeries, are full of birds. If an enemy comes near they all squawk noisily to scare it away and to alert others to danger. This way, when the parents go to hunt, there are plenty of other eyes watching their chick.

Masked lapwings get very angry if their eggs or chicks are under threat. They swoop down on anyone or anything that might upset their grassy nest. Sharp spurs that poke out of their wings help them fight off any attackers.

Masked lapwing

Magpies

Dive-bombing daddies

Magpies fiercely protect their nests when they have chicks. They even dive-bomb people to scare them away. Scientists have found that magpie mothers and fathers don't usually dive-bomb people they see passing by all the time. They mostly only dive-bomb strangers, because they see them as threats.

Eagle

Winged wanderers

Brahminy kite

Some birds are perfectly suited to flying long distances and may spend most of their lives "on the wing". It can be tiring to fly such a long way, but soaring on wind currents uses far less energy than flapping the wings.

Albatrosses can soar for hours and hours — sometimes all day long. They usually only land to lay eggs and raise their young chicks.

Seabirds that spend a lot of time fishing over the ocean need to be able to soar for a long time. Brahminy kites use warm air currents to float over the oceans, looking for the glint of fish below.

Albatross

Australian pelicans

Pelican "planes"...

A flock of pelicans is known as a squadron — the same name as a group of aeroplanes. Pelicans are the largest flying birds in Australia and their outstretched wings may measure up to 3 metres, which is longer than a person is tall.

Budgerigars

Birds that fly from one place to another to search for food are called migratory birds. Some fly in huge flocks, from as far away as the Arctic Circle, stopping only to eat and sleep. These birds need safe places in each country where they can stop to rest and eat.

Bountiful budgies

Wild budgies fly in huge, screeching flocks across the outback. They eat grass seeds and will fly wherever the grass is seeding. You may have seen pet budgies in all sorts of colours, but in the wild they are always green and yellow.

Life in the undergrowth

Lyrebird

Some birds are poor fliers and are known as "ground birds". They choose to live on land and rarely fly, even if they are able to. Some of the most interesting ground birds are known as megapodes, which means "big feet".

You may have seen brush-turkeys pecking around your garden or in parks. They use their strong legs to scratch together a high nest of leaf litter. Brush-turkeys need to keep the nest at just the right warmth for the eggs to hatch.

Australian brush-turkey

Malleefowl

Male malleefowl also build high nests of dirt and leaves on the ground. They jab their beaks into the soil to test the nest's heat because, like brush-turkeys, they need to keep the nest warm.

Emus

Bird speedsters

Emus and cassowaries may not be able to fly, but they can run very fast. Emus can sprint at 50 kilometres an hour, almost as fast as a car can drive in suburban streets.

Southern cassowary

The huge, glossy black cassowary lives in the tropical rainforests of north Queensland. It crashes through the rainforest, pushing vines out of the way with the bony "horn" on its head, which is called a casque.

I headbutt plants out of the way!

Spotted nightjar

Hide & seek

The spotted nightjar is a very shy bird that nests on the ground. To help it avoid being eaten by predators, it has speckled brown and black feathers so it can blend in with the colours of leaves and bark on the ground.

Australian brush-turkey

Shady characters

Some beautiful birds live in Australia's moist shady forests. Most peck up fruit from the forest floor or dig in the leaf litter for insects.

Lyrebirds build platforms of leaves on the damp forest floor, where they dance and shake their lacy tails to attract a mate.

Superb lyrebird

In the forest, you might hear birds well before you can see them. The calls of the spotted catbird and the eastern yellow robin are two common birdsongs in wet forests.

Spotted catbird

Eastern yellow robin

Rose-crowned fruit-dove

Superb seed spreaders

Fruit-eating birds like the emerald dove and the pretty rose-crowned fruit-dove have an important job to do in the forest. They help spread the seeds of rainforest plants, which stick to their beaks and feet and are passed out in the birds' poo. This helps the rainforest continue to grow.

Emerald dove

Eclectus parrots

We live in tree hollows.

Eclectus parrots lay their eggs and raise their chicks in hollow trees in the forest. Green males and red females look very different. In fact, scientists once thought they were two different types of parrot.

Australian king-parrot

Crimson rosella

Noisy forest birds

The largest cockatoo in Australia, the black and red palm cockatoo, lives in wet forests. It eats the nuts of pandanus palms. Other seed- and nut-eating birds of the forest are crimson rosellas and king-parrots. All of these birds are very colourful and are also very noisy.

Palm cockatoo

Out in the ocean air

Silver gull

Silver gull

Some birds prefer to live by the sea, where they feed on fish and other marine animals. Often these birds live in large groups and hunt for food together, squabbling loudly over their share.

Gulls are cheeky scavengers. They usually follow people fishing to feed on fish scraps. You may even have to shoo them away from your fish and chips at the beach.

Pied oystercatcher

Others prefer to walk along the beach alone, searching for food. You may have seen red-legged pied oystercatchers hunting on the beach for their dinner. They poke about in the sand to find pipis, which they then force open with their sharp beaks.

A regal surface snatcher

White-bellied sea-eagle

The osprey and the white-bellied sea-eagle are majestic birds of prey that build their nests by the sea. The white-bellied sea-eagle is the second-largest bird of prey in Australia, after the wedge-tailed eagle. It dives down from the sky to pluck fish up from the water.

Red-footed boobies

Boobies and gannets are all seabirds that nest in large, squawking colonies on Australia's coasts and islands. Because a booby must dive down into the water to catch fish, its eyes and its beak are joined together in a type of "mask" and it has no nostrils. This stops water shooting up the bird's nose when it dives.

Take your tern

Black-naped tern

Sooty tern

Some of the most commonly seen birds on beaches, islands and coral cays are terns. There are many types of tern and some migrate to Australia from other shores. Some are endangered, so when you go to the beach, be careful to stay away from any nesting terns.

Swamp & lagoon lovers

Magpie goose

Royal spoonbill

Rufous night heron

The water in many lagoons and rivers is fresh, not salty. Land animals need freshwater to live and wetlands like Kakadu attract hundreds of water-loving birds and waders, which feast on fish, water weeds and insects.

Ducks, swans and native geese, such as magpie geese, share their watery habitat with waders like herons, black-necked storks, spoonbills and ibis. An ibis can eat around one-quarter of its own body weight daily — that's a lot of fish!

Pelicans also travel a long way to feed in the wetlands. They scoop up fish in their huge, pouch-like beaks then swallow them headfirst.

Australian pelicans

Pied cormorant

Hung out to dry

Darters and cormorants swim underwater to sneak up on fish and yabbies. Their feathers are not waterproof so when they come out of the water they have to dry their outstretched wings in the sun before they can fly off.

Darter

Some wetlands are only wet for part of the year, following heavy rains. Huge numbers of birds may fly in to eat and nest there at that time. Once the waterholes dry up, the birds fly off again in search of other wetland habitats.

Magpie geese

Intermediate egret

Pied heron

Long legs & strange sounds

Long-legged waders, such as herons and egrets, stalk slowly through wetlands, spearing fish and snakes with their long beaks. They nest in large colonies that are noisy with honks, groans and croaks. The call of the great-billed heron is even said to sound like a bull's roar.

Princess parrot

Some like it hot

Emu

Birds live just about anywhere, even in very dry desert areas. Of course, desert birds need to find ways to save water, so many of them get most of the water they need from eating seeds or insects. Some live in burrows to stay cool, and others hunt only at night.

The princess parrot is a rarely seen parrot that lives in the dry inland. It is one of Australia's prettiest parrots and eats the seeds of spinifex bushes as well as flowers and fruits.

Galahs are cheeky pink and grey birds that live all over Australia. In the desert, they rarely see rain, but when it does finally pour down, they like to splash and play in the puddles.

Galahs

Chirruping wedgebill

A call like a whip

The chirruping wedgebill is a type of aridland whipbird that flies alone or in small family groups. It can often be heard chirruping a trilling "tsiep-TSIEER" song from the top of wattle trees or saltbushes.

Spinifex pigeon

Spinifex pigeons are usually seen perching on rocks or searching for seeds in dry land close to waterholes across inland Australia. Their orange and black speckled feathers help them blend in with the red rocks and dust.

I blend in with the desert colours.

Dainty desert-dwellers

White-winged fairy-wren

Crimson chat

Zebra finch

Small desert birds like finches, firetails, chats and the white-winged fairy-wren usually stay close to water. They flutter their wings and ruffle their feathers to stay cool in the sweltering heat.

Woodland wonders

Magpie

Yellow-tufted honeyeater

All sorts of birds make their homes in the bush and woodlands, from shrieking colourful cockatoos to kookaburras and honeyeaters. Some build grassy or leafy nests low in the branches and others nest in tree hollows.

The yellow-tufted honeyeater is an endangered bird that lives in gum tree woodlands. It makes a cup-shaped nest of woven leaves, bark and cobwebs to raise its babies.

The red-browed finch uses grass to make its bottle-shaped nest in the shrubby or grassy undergrowth of woodlands and bushlands.

Red-browed finch

kings of the bush

Australia has two kinds of kookaburra, the laughing kookaburra and the blue-winged kookaburra. Kookaburras are really the largest of the kingfishers. Can you make their cackling koo-ah-ah-kook-kook-kook call?

Laughing kookaburra

Blue-winged kookaburra

44

Sulphur-crested cockatoos

Yellow-tailed black-cockatoo

Gang-gang cockatoo

clever & curious

Australia is famous for its many cockatoo species. Cockatoos are curious, clever birds. Unlike other parrots, they have crests on the top of their heads. They raise or lower their crests to "talk" to each other or to show interest or alarm.

Living with birds

Little penguins

People and birds often share the same habitat on the coast, in parks and gardens, and in backyards and cities. Humans can help birds by making sure we keep beaches clean, don't cut down trees (especially old trees) and keep our pets away from birds.

Birdwatching

It is great fun watching and photographing birds at wetlands and in national parks, but take care not to get so close that you frighten birds off their nests or away from their natural habitat.

Many birds need hollow trees to make their nests or homes in, so we shouldn't cut down trees, even dead ones.

Scaly-breasted lorikeet

Rainbow lorikeet

Yummy native food

Native Australian birds are used to eating the sweet nectar, nuts or flowers of Australian plants. Planting native trees like bottlebrushes and grevilleas in your yard can help give birds a source of food.

Ready, set, catch!

It is fun to see gulls and pelicans feed on fish at the beach. Keeping beaches clean from litter and thrown-away fishing line will help protect our beach birds.

Australian pelicans

Dog

Crimson rosella

Feral cat

Look after birds

Some birds can become quite tame around humans. However, we need to make sure that being around humans doesn't hurt them. Never feed bread or meat to native birds, and keep pet dogs and cats locked in at night so they don't hunt birds.

ANCESTOR A relative from long ago or a species that a modern animal evolved from.

ANCIENT Millions of years old.

AVOID Keep away from.

BREED Make babies.

CAROLLER Someone that sings joyfully.

CAY Small island.

COLONY A group of birds that live together.

ECHOLOCATION To sense an object by sending out sounds then listening to the echoes that bounce off the object.

EMBRYO A very early stage in a baby bird's development when it is very small and still needs to grow inside the egg.

ENDANGERED At risk of becoming extinct.

FLOCK A group of birds.

HABITAT The place where an animal or plant lives or grows.

HATCH When a baby bird breaks through its egg.

MATE When a male animal transfers special cells to a female's eggs, which causes young ones to develop.

MELODY A song.

MIGRATE To go from one country or place to another.

MIMIC To copy the looks or behaviour of another animal.

MOULTING When feathers fall out to be replaced by new feathers.

PREDATOR An animal that hunts and eats animals.

PREEN To clean or groom.

PREY An animal that gets eaten by another animal. Can also mean to hunt.

RARELY Not common.

ROOKERY A place where a colony of birds comes together to make and raise babies.

ROOST When birds sleep or rest.

SCAVENGER An animal that eats dead animals.

SPECIES A group of organisms that can breed to make babies.

SWOOP Suddenly dropping down through the air.

TALONS Sharp claws.

TRILL A high-pitched, vibrating sound.

UNIQUE One of a kind.